W*aimea*
A BIG ISLAND TREASURE

Limited Edition
thirty five hundred copies

1869

Aloha My Friend,

I am pleased to present to you this beautiful book, "Waimea". As you will see and read, this small township is alive with a mix of magic and majesty, wildlife and calm living, expansiveness and small-town intimacy.

Nestled in the saddle of two of our magnificent volcanoes – Mauna Kea and Kohala – we look in one direction to see a snow-capped peak, and simply turn around to see lush green rain forests. Cattle, horses, and sheep graze contentedly in wide open pastures, while farmers harvest fresh green vegetables laden with early morning dew.

For many years, this area with its cool, misty weather has been known as a place of healing, retreat and regeneration. It is no accident that our renowned North Hawaii Community Hospital sits inWaimea, on a sacred site that was once a gathering place more than one thousand years for people who celebrated peace and good will.

I love driving up into the misty foothills of Waimea. We often pass through double rainbows as we wind our way upland from the coast to the cool 3000' elevation. Much of my work here on Hawaii Island is centered in Waimea and many of my dreams have come true here.

I hope you enjoy "Waimea" as much as I have, and I invite you to visit us whenever you can. I believe you will be embraced by its magic as I am. Until that time, I wish you and yours a peaceful and joyful 2005 Holiday Season.

Dreaming on,

Earl E. Bakken

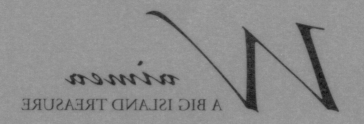

Waimea

A BIG ISLAND TREASURE

Limited Edition
thirty five hundred copies

1869

Aloha My Friend,

I am pleased to present to you this beautiful book, "Waimea". As you will see and read, this small township is alive with a mix of magic and majesty, wildlife and calm living, expansiveness and small-town intimacy.

Nestled in the saddle of two of our magnificent volcanoes – Mauna Kea and Kohala – we look in one direction to see a snow-capped peak, and simply turn around to see lush green rain forests. Cattle, horses, and sheep graze contentedly in wide open pastures, while farmers harvest fresh green vegetables laden with early morning dew.

For many years, this area with its cool, misty weather has been known as a place of healing, retreat and regeneration. It is no accident that our renowned North Hawaii Community Hospital sits in Waimea, on a sacred site that was once a gathering place more than one thousand years for people who celebrated peace and good will.

I love driving up into the misty foothills of Waimea. We often pass through double rainbows as we wind our way upland from the coast to the cool 3000' elevation. Much of my work here on Hawaii Island is centered in Waimea and many of my dreams have come true here.

I hope you enjoy "Waimea" as much as I have, and I invite you to visit us whenever you can. I believe you will be embraced by its magic as I am. Until that time, I wish you and yours a peaceful and joyful 2005 Holiday Season.

Dreaming on,

Earl E. Bakken

With appreciation to those
who made publication of this book possible

Mr. & Mrs. Earl Bakken

MacArthur & Company

Waikoloa Beach Marriott

Hilton Waikoloa Village

PHOTOGRAPHY and DESIGN
Linda Ching

Moʻoleo Chapter
Lynn Cook

Cover photo:
Ikua Purdy Statue
Courtesy of Paniolo Preservation Society
Photo by Linda Ching

Waimea
A BIG ISLAND TREASURE

Photography © copyright Linda Ching
Library of Congress Control Number 2005924851
ISBN 0961989181

Printed in Hong Kong

Contents

Acknowledgements

Thank you and aloha to the beautiful people of Waimea who grace these pages. My heartfelt appreciation to the sponsors for placing your faith in this labor of love and making this book possible. Mahalo Dr. Billy Bergin for sharing your knowledge and so generously allowing me to photograph your remarkable collection of paniolo artifacts. To Sheila Davies for proofreading this and every one of my books, thank you for your keen eye for detail, for always finding the perfect word to finish my sentences and for the patience that could only come from a true friend.

Preface

Was Eden a divine garden, a metaphor, a state of mind or a place of longing in our hearts? When the missionaries arrived in the remote Waimea uplands of Hawai'i Island, the idyllic paradise of Genesis may not have readily come to mind. It was colder back then they say, famous for the piercing Kīpu'upu'u wind and rain. Its misty and rugged terrain alive with a mystic beat of wild hearts summoned a breed who followed their own course – roughriders, adventurers, visionaries, artists, lovers of beauty, those in search of a more authentic life. These were heartier souls who could withstand the inevitable changes time would bring. The missionaries brought one of the first waves of change. Natives seemed to embrace their teachings readily and adopted a name for their mythic Garden – Edena Nani, Beautiful Eden.

In the past months, I'd often sit with my camera in hand waiting for the first light of day and reflected on how natural it would have been for early Hawaiians to relate to a paradise garden. Surely, in these islands, so often referred to as Paradise, Waimea seems to be especially blessed.

What can I tell you about Waimea? First, it has two names. It will always be Waimea to the old timers. But there were several towns with the same name so as it grew, the post office and zip code took on another name for it - Kamuela. But this is the least of what makes the town different. Here flourished a paniolo (cowboy) culture that became uniquely Hawaiian in spirit. The living legacy of this culture is evident in the proud faces of the children. A sweet abundance flourishes from the fertile land. On certain days the rolling hills emanate a vibrant green that can take your breath away.

It was my good fortune to have the opportunity to indulge awhile and take in a special place that seemed to skip in time to my own inner beat. Here is a tribute to an island treasure and to the people who call heavenly Waimea home.

Linda Ching
Honolulu 2005

1

Mo'olelo

The story...

A unique and colorful history

JOHN PARKER
RIGHT: MANA HALE WINDOW,
PARKER RANCH HISTORICAL HOMES

Moʻolelo of the Mountains

Living an ocean and a continent away from paradise, in Newton, Massachusetts, John Palmer Parker was only two years old when Captain George Vancouver delivered the first cattle to the Hawaiian Islands. This small boy had no way of knowing that one day he would own and run a cattle ranch. Nor did he expect that his fame and fortune would be found in a place then barely known as the Sandwich Isles.

At age eighteen he went to sea on a whaling ship. By the early 1800's he was disenchanted with the sailing life. His first glimpse of the Big Island captured his imagination. He jumped ship, hid in the underbrush and watched his vessel sail away. He learned the Hawaiian language, was befriended by King Kamehameha I, and set out on his path to make Hawaii home. John Parker began building his empire at the time his friend, the great monarch Kamehameha died. The first missionaries arrived and the island's old religion was set aside. A written language was presented to the islanders, the bible was translated into Hawaiian and island life was forever changed.

"On the grassy plateau, Kamehameha I had liberated the cattle that were Vancouver's precious gift. There roamed the wild progeny, hunted for their hides by reckless Mexican cowboys, whose riding was soon matched by that of Hawaiians as fearless as they."

Emma Lyons Doyle

The big-horned cattle, gifted to the king, understandably terrified
the local population. Accounts vary, but the cattle (called pipi),
long kept on a ship, lowered into the water, and dragged to shore
by outrigger canoe, were most certainly in a very bad mood.
A second voyage brought more longhorns. To insure offspring, a
kapu was put out, no cattle were to be killed. Soon missionary
Lorenzo Lyons, in charge of the Waimea Mission, described the
area as a "big cattle pen". Bulls ravaged gardens and boldly
walked through the native homes. The answer? Mexican
vaqueros came with their horses to teach the cowboy arts to the
natives. It was love at first ride. The term vaquero became the
Hawaiian Paniolo, dashing, daring and larger than life.

The lyric poet
of mountain country

His welcome to the remote district of Waimea was as dismal as the highland chill that greeted him that day, but the young missionary from Massachusetts kept the faith and prayed for the natives who fled at the sight of him like frightened deer and for the others who jeered and ridiculed him with shameless gestures. In his journal from the early days of 1832, Reverend Lorenzo Lyons wrote, *"Various things are rumored about us. One is that we wish to get children to school in order to kill them by putting them in barrels."* Others thought the missionaries went to their houses at night to kill people for their brains and blood for the sacrament.

In time, his tireless efforts won their respect and trust, his dedication to the people opened their hearts to a love that became legendary. Lyons had a natural knack for rhythm, and poetry was in his soul. With a gifted command of the Hawaiian language, he translated and wrote hundreds of hymnals and songs for those he ministered. With much aloha they named him as one of their own; *Ka Maukua Laiana, Hoku Mele o ka Aina Mauna, Father Lyons, Lyric Poet of the Mountain Country.*

RIGHT: REVEREND LORENZO LYONS

*"And you, Hawaiians of 1832, living your days as your ances-
tors had lived theirs, on the inland plains, the rugged fastness of
Hawaii, recording your thoughts in no journal, but thinking
them, nevertheless: when there suddenly flashed into your lives
these beings, with strange language, strange dress, mysterious
motives and weird customs, what thought you?"*

Emma Lyons Doyle's reflections on her missionary grandfather, the beloved
Reverend Lorenzo Lyons' arrival to Waimea in 1832.

ABOVE: HEADBOARD DETAIL.
1870'S AMERICAN VICTORIAN GOTHIC STYLE

RIGHT: MANA HALE KOA WOOD BEDROOM,
PARKER RANCH HISTORIC HOMES

The Long Ride Home

In 1848 the Great Mahele allowed foreign land ownership. John Palmer Parker bought the land he ranched and more. He hired more paniolo cowboys and expanded his herd. He created what was to become the largest private cattle ranch in the U.S., encompassing over 500,000 acres — when Hawaii became a territory and later a state. His home was reported as "stylish, with windows, board floor, and cowhide carpets." His cattle pens were solidly built of stone walls. Then came a saddle house, a blacksmith shop, a barn, a meathouse, smoke-house and a dairy. He and his Hawaiian wife, Kipikane, grand daughter of Kamehameha, raised three children.

What was once a windswept, desolate mountain became a vibrant center for cattle ranching and rodeo riding, unequaled by any state or country. Kamuela, Waimea, and Waikoloa became names of legend in the world of riding and roping. Four "dark-skinned" men traveled first by ship and then train to the Cheyenne Round-up, only to be given unbroken horses and looks of disbelief from the 'wild west' cowboys. They did what they were trained to do, ride hard and ride well. One, Ikua Purdy, became World Champion. On their return, the islands erupted with celebrations and parties, so many it is told, that it took six months for them to get back to work on the Big Island. The Hawaiian Paniolo became the legend that lives on today.

*I*kua Purdy…number one cowboy in the world. The legend lives and its memory celebrated in song of how two Parker Ranch cowboys stunned the world and placed first and third in the 1908 Wyoming World Championship Rodeo.

Kaulana Ikuwa me Kaʻaua, lā
Na ʻeu kīpuka ʻili
Na āiwaiwa ʻo Eulopa, lā
Waimea e ka ʻeu
Ka ua Kīpuʻupuʻu
Kahua Waiomina

Famous are Ikuwa and Kaʻaua
Both mischievous with the lariat
Both experts in Europe
Waimea full of gusto
The hard rain named Kīpuʻupuʻu
To the stadium of Wyoming

Waiomina (Wyoming), Helen Parker

ABOVE: IKUA PURDY HAT. DR. BILLY BERGIN COLLECTION
RIGHT: REPLICA OF PANIOLO HUT, PARKER RANCH MUSEUM

Two more John Palmer Parkers (the second and third) continued the dynasty, eventually passing it on to Thelma Parker Smart and her son, Richard Smart. Today the Parker Ranch historic homes of Mana Hale and Puuopelu are living testaments to the gracious life created in the heart of Hawaiian cowboy country. World travelers, dignitaries, great explorers and even royalty were welcomed and entertained by generations of Parkers. The warmth and welcome still stretch from Waikoloa to Waimea. Visitors feel the mana (spirit) that first attracted John Palmer Parker and has anchored the community from the first wandering cattle days.

MANA HALE EXTERIOR
PARKER RANCH HISTORICAL HOMES

ABOVE: PUUOPELU GARDENS

RIGHT: PUUOPELU, PARKER RANCH HISTORICAL HOMES

2

Kuaola

The verdant mountain…

Where all things flourish

KE OLA MAU LOA CHURCH
CHURCH ROW, WAIMEA TOWN

ABOVE: MORNING GLORY
RIGHT: DRYLAND OPEN FIELD

Beautiful Waimea, my place of birth, Famous for the Kīpuʻupuʻu rain
The three beautiful mountains, You are ever my fancy.
Waimea Ku'u One Hanau, Alice Nakalelau

SUNRISE OVER MAUNA KEA

*D*onnie DeSilva, Parker Ranch cowboy, bronco buster of the breaking pen, retired his trusted horse Blue to pasture at the time of his retirement. Blue, who is white, was blue as a young colt. "I met him when he was 3 and now he's 25. It's a matter of trust and respect with us."

Saddle making and repair is Donnie's second career. Through the hands from the heart…with a steady touch he tames the leather as he once tamed the horses. "I just do it the way I was taught." he says, "You can't beat the old ways."

4s SADDLERY
and boot repair

NALAN
7868

RIGHT: IN THE SHADE OF AN OLD JACARANDA TREE,
WAGON WHEELS REMIND US OF DAYS GONES BY.

DAY BREAKING OVER MAUNA KEA, MANA ROAD

Waimea visionary…

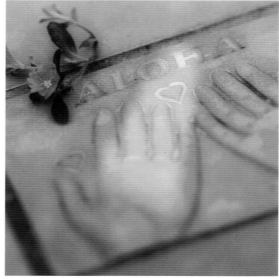

Dr. Earl E. Bakken…when he was nine, he dreamed of Frankenstein. It was real, the fact that life restoration could be done with electricity. He knew, "when electricity flows, we're alive; when it doesn't, we're not." In the garage, he wired things together, invented, questioned and re-invented. His mother encouraged him, especially when he invented a phone that connected her to a friend's house across town. Erector sets, electric trains and Lincoln Logs were transformed into new inventions. One robot blinked its eyes. The next one was a moving Samurai warrior.

His garage became the first world headquarters for Medtronics, a company that today still leads the world in medical technology by providing solutions to people with chronic disease. With transistors, he invented a portable pacemaker to keep newborn babies alive while holes in their hearts were repaired. He perfected the pacemaker. In the 1960's, there were 50 ordered; today 690,000 are sold worldwide. Beyond mechanical inventions, this man dreamed of educating and inspiring children, giving them a dream of their own.

It was later in life he found peaceful respite in Hawaii, but his dreams inspired by the five mountains surrounding Waimea kept coming. He turned them into realities - learning museums, teaching libraries, health maps and heart-brain medicine and a hospital for Waimea that serves as a beacon for blending high-tech and high-touch techniques in contemporary medicine.

He shares his dreams with students of all ages. When asked if he is going to duplicate his realized and successful dream of the Five Mountains Hawaii health and wellness community, blended medicine, and the Waimea North Hawaii Community Hospital with the rest of the world, he answers, "I don't need to. Now it's your turn. You take the dream and run with it."

L. Cook

Lokahi...
The Unity of Five Mountains

Lokahi is unity, a balance in life - mind, body, spirit, nature, family, and community. The power of the five mountains surrounding Waimea brought ancient voyagers across thousands of miles and thousands of years, drawn by the healing energy.

Mauna Kea ~ White Mountain
Mauna Loa ~ Long Mountain
Hualalai ~ Nursing Mother, High Chieftess
Kohala ~ Place of Destiny
Haleakala ~ House of the Sun

It is this power that fills Tutu's House, a wellness resource center, where the community can take ownership of knowledge to maintain their health and well-being. It is from this energy Earl's Garage was born - a place where young inventors can quench their thirst for knowledge and explore new worlds. After school, Dr. Earl Bakken's Just Think Mobile cruises the highways and byways of learning taking students to new realms of creativity. Wellness fills the North Hawaii Community Hospital, where fresh mountain breezes heal the body, lavender heals the soul and cutting edge technology blends it all in unity.

L. Cook

ABOVE: INTERNATIONAL
OBSERVATORIES ON SNOW CAPPED MAUNA KEA

LEFT: MAUNA LOA PROVIDES A WINTER BACKDROP
FOR WAIMEA'S GRASSY PLAINS

The Just Think Bus on its way to ignite the imagination
of Waimea's students. "Never stop dreaming" is the rally cry
that drives the community into the future.

3

Nā keiki hoʻolei kīpuka ʻili

The children who throw lassos…

The paniolo legacy lives on in the spirit of Waimea's rodeo kids.

ANNUAL KEIKI COMPETITION

LEFT: CHAMPIONSHIP MUTTON BUSTING

ABOVE: RODEO SPECTATORS
LEFT: TROLLY HORSE TAKES A MOMENT FOR A LITTLE SHUT EYE.

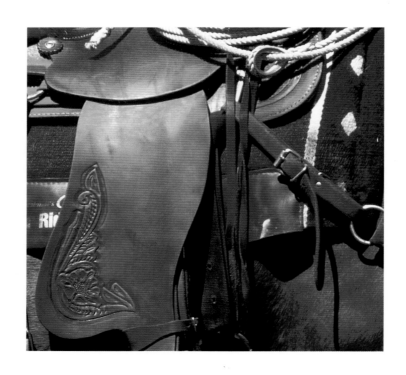

ABOVE: FLAG BEARERS AT A HIGH SCHOOL RODEO CEREMONY
RIGHT: PINK RHINESTONE COWGIRL

ANTIQUE CHILD'S SADDLE, COURTESY OF DR. BILLY BERGIN

RIGHT: Kamehana, budding cowgirl, competed in her first rodeo just after her first birthday. You could say it's in her blood. She's sixth generation paniolo.

What does it take to make a good cowgirl? "Guts and a lot of heart," she says.

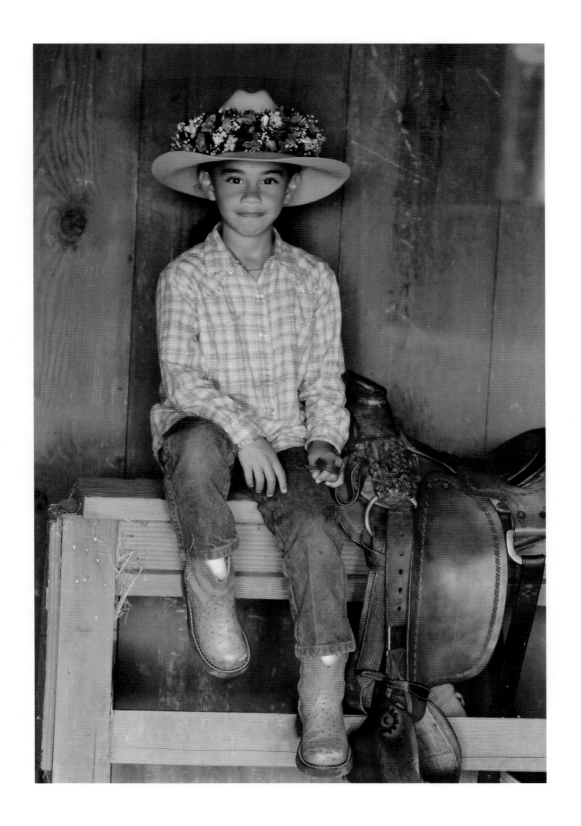

ABOVE: THE LITTLEST COWBOY
RIGHT: PRICKLY CACTUS SMILES

4
A'ala
The fragrant…

Aloha ʻāina – loving the land brings forth fragrant gifts in abundance and a banquet for the senses.

KAMUELA LETTUCE FARM

TOMATOES RIPENING ON
LALAMILO ROAD

Waimea Tomato Salad

Ingredients
  12 oz. sliced Waimea tomatoes
  4 oz. sliced fresh mozzarella cheese
  4 oz. thinly sliced Maui onions
  2 oz. grated Parmesan cheese
  4 oz. basil vinaigrette
  1 julienne basil

Basil Vinaigrette
  5 oz. olive oil
  2.5 oz. white wine vinegar
  2 tsp. minced shallots
  2 tsp. minced basil
  2 tsp. grated Parmesan cheese
  1/8 oz. Dijon mustard
  Salt to taste

Method:
  Arrange tomatoes & mozzarella cheese in a circle.
  Top with Maui onions, basil, vinaigrette &
    grated Parmesan cheese

Basil Vinaigrette:
  Place all ingredients in a stainless steel bowl,
  except olive oil. Whip together & add olive oil.
  Season with salt.

  Yield: 4 servings

From the kitchen for Patrick Saito, Chef de Cuisine
Waikoloa Beach Marriott Resort

Waimea Strawberry Caramel Custard

Ingredients
   1 1/2 cup heavy cream
   1 1/2 cup milk
   3/4 cup brown sugar, firmly packed
   7 each whole eggs
   1 tsp. vanilla extract
   a pinch of salt

   Caramel bottom:
   1 cup granulated sugar
   1/4 cup water

Method:
   Caramel Bottom:
   Mix granulated sugar and water in a medium saucepot. With a clean
   pastry brush, wipe sides down with water. Bring to a boil and reduce to a
   caramel color. Take off heat and pour into 8 oz. bake-proof ramekins. Let cool.

   Custard filling:
   Mix eggs and brown sugar in a mixing bowl. Add in cream and milk slowly. Add in salt and
   vanilla extract.   Strain through a fine sieve and pour over cooled caramel. Bake in a water bath
   at 325 degrees for about 25-30 minutes or until set. Chill at least four hours. Serve with
   Waimea Strawberries.

   Yield: 4 – 6 servings

From the kitchen of Executive Pastry Chef Ashley Nakano
Hilton Waikoloa Village

Waimea Beef Salad

Ingredients
 1 lb flank steak
 4 oz. Waimea baby greens
 4 oz. sliced cucumbers
 8 oz. cherry tomatoes
 2 oz. thinly sliced onions
 1 oz. julienne basil
 6 oz. Thai vinaigrette
 12 to 16 mint leaves
 1 oz. minced garlic

Thai Vinaigrette:
 6 oz. peanut oil
 2 oz. rice wine vinegar
 1 oz. fresh lime juice
 1/8 oz. minced garlic
 1/8 oz. minced ginger
 1/8 oz. chopped mint
 1/8 oz. chopped basil
 1/16 oz. fish sauce
 1 pc. Hawaiian chili pepper, chopped fine
 1 oz. shoyu
 1 oz. sugar

Method:
Rub garlic on steak, Grill to desired doneness & slice. Arrange greens on plate, add cherry tomatoes
& cucumbers. Place sliced flank steak on greens. Top with basil, onions, mint leaves & Thai Vinaigrette.
Place all ingredients in a blender except peanut oil. Blend on medium Add peanut oil slowly.
Yield: 4 servings

From the kitchen of Patrick Saito, Chef de Cuisine
Waikoloa Beach Marriott Resort

Kamuela Tomato, Buffalo Mozzarella on Baby Greens

Ingredients
  4 Vine ripened Kamuela tomatoes
  3 pcs buffalo mozzarella
  Assorted baby greens (lola rosa,
  baby romaine, red oak)
  1/2 thinly shaved red onion

Dressing
  8 oz. extra virgin olive oil
  5 oz. balsamic vinegar
  Fresh ground back pepper
  1/2 oz. dried oregano, ground
  A few dried fennel seeds, ground

Method:

Dressing
  Combine all ingredients and mix well.
  No salt is necessary, balsamic vinegar
  usually has enough in it.

Salad
  Slice tomato into 4 slices.
  Slice buffalo mozzarella into 3 or 4 slices.
  Place baby lettuce leaves on the plate.
  Stack the tomato and cheese, layering them.
  Place the shaved red onions around tomato.
  Drizzle dressing over entire salad.

  Yield: 4 servings

  From the kitchen of Chef Kenny Omiya
  Hilton Waikoloa Village

Waimea Strawberry Tart

Ingredients
  3 – 4 in. tart shells
  15 pcs. Waimea strawberries
  9 oz. pastry cream
  Garnish

Pastry Cream
  4 oz. milk
  4 oz. heavy cream
  2.5 oz. sugar
  1 tsp. vanilla
  1 whole egg
  1 oz. cornstarch
  1 oz. butter

Method:
  Bring milk, cream, vanilla & sugar to a boil in a heavy
  saucepan, lower heat. Mix egg & cornstarch, whip
  into cream mixture, and add butter, let cool. Fill tart
  shell with pastry cream, top with fresh strawberries
  and garnish.

  Yield: 3 servings

From the kitchen of Modesto Bala, Baker
Waikoloa Beach Marriott Resort

a hui hou aku — until we meet again...

PAU